HOW TO START YOUR OWN CANDLE-MAKING BUSINESS

From Hobby To Profit

Candle Crafting Tips and Entrepreneurial Insights for Success

Dr. Elias Elizabeth

1

CHAPTER ONE

Introduction

Candle-making is an old skill that has developed throughout time, from a requirement for light to a creative and enjoyable art form. In recent years, the skill of candle manufacturing has grown in popularity not just as a pastime, but also as a possible business opportunity.

This transition from a simple leisure to a full-fledged company requires a thorough grasp of the craft, market dynamics, and the use of numerous methods to produce high-quality candles.

The Art And Joy Of Candle Production

Candlemaking is more than a functional skill; it is a form of creative expression that both makers and consumers enjoy. Melting wax, selecting perfumes, and sculpting forms enable people to express their creativity. Whether making candles as presents for loved ones or producing one-of-a-kind items for personal use, the art of candle making is a relaxing and rewarding experience.

One of the most pleasant features of this profession is the diversity it provides. Candlemakers may create an infinite number of designs by experimenting with various kinds of wax, colors, smells, and molds.

The choices range from standard taper candles to elaborately formed pillars and novelty candles, the only limit being one's creativity. This variety draws people from many walks of life, adding to the popularity of candle manufacturing as a pastime.

From Hobbyist To Entrepreneur: A Transition Journey

For many people, what starts as a simple pastime becomes a passionate endeavor that inspires them to share their products with a larger audience. The road from candlemaking enthusiast to business is an interesting one, filled with both obstacles and benefits. This change often includes increasing production, building an online or physical presence, and creating a brand identity.

Aspiring candle makers must carefully manage the shift, combining their passion for the art with the practicalities of operating a company.

This involves creating a specialized workplace, acquiring high-quality materials, and comprehending the legal and regulatory elements of selling candles. Furthermore, developing a brand presence via social media platforms and local marketplaces is critical for contacting prospective consumers.

Understanding The Candle Market

To be successful in the candle-making industry, you must have a thorough awareness of the candle market. This includes monitoring consumer trends, determining target demographics, and keeping current on industry developments. The candle market is broad, catering to a wide variety of interests and demands.

Consumers may pursue candles for a variety of reasons, including aromatherapy, home design, and religious rituals. Understanding these various needs enables candlemakers to design their goods for particular market segments. Furthermore, remaining current on popular scents, colors, and trends ensures that the candles manufactured reflect current customer tastes.

Making Quality Candles: Techniques And Tips

The capacity to produce high-quality goods is crucial to a successful candle-making business. This includes understanding numerous methods and adopting ideas to improve the visual appeal, burn duration, and smell strength of the candles.

Choosing the appropriate wax is an essential part of candlemaking. Different waxes, such as paraffin, soy, and beeswax, have unique properties that affect the finished product. Understanding the properties of each wax type allows candle manufacturers to make educated judgments depending on the intended results.

Another important aspect of candle production is choosing the right aroma. The aroma of a candle is important to its market appeal, and mastering the skill of fragrance mixing may help a candle producer stand out. Experimentation with essential oils and fragrance oils enables the production of distinctive aromas that appeal to clients.

Molding and shaping methods enhance the visual attractiveness of candles. The method used, whether standard molds or hand-poured handmade patterns, may have an impact on the overall appearance of the completed product. The attention to detail in areas like as wick placement, color dispersion, and surface polish improves the quality of the candles.

Furthermore, knowing the science of candle manufacture, such as the right wax-to-fragrance ratios and the ideal wick size for various candle sizes, provides a consistent and high-quality finished product. Techniques must be tested and refined regularly to ensure ongoing progress.

To summarize, the route from hobbyist candle maker to successful enterprise requires a strong respect for the art and pleasure of candle making. This change requires a thorough awareness of the market, a dedication to producing high-quality goods, and the flexibility to adapt to customers' ever-changing demands. Whether making candles for a therapeutic pastime or as a commercial enterprise, the art of candle-making continues to enchant people with its limitless opportunities for creativity and expression.

CHAPTER TWO
Essential Tools And Materials
For Candlemaking

Candlemaking is a creative and gratifying activity that has grown in popularity in recent years. Whether you're a hobbyist or want to establish your own candle-making company, having the correct equipment and supplies is essential for success. Here, we'll look at the main supplies you'll need to make gorgeous, high-quality candles.

Wax Selection

Choosing the correct wax is essential for the candle-making process. There are many forms of wax available, including paraffin, soy, beeswax, and palm wax. Each variety has its distinct qualities, such as burning duration, smell throw, and look. When deciding on the right wax for your candles, keep your tastes and intended result in mind.

Wick Varieties

Wicks play an important part in influencing how a candle burns. Choosing the appropriate wick size and substance enables optimal combustion and avoids problems like as tunneling or uneven melting. Wicks exist in many sizes and materials, including cotton, wood, and hemp. Experimenting with different wick alternatives can help you get the right flame and burn for your candles.

Fragrances And Colors

Add perfumes and colors to your candles to enhance their attractiveness. Fragrance oils, which come in a variety of aromas, add to the environment created by your candles. Similarly, choosing the proper hue or mix of colors adds visual interest to your candles. To get a harmonious effect, consider the aroma and color compatibility of the wax you choose.

Mold And Containers

Molds and containers come in a variety of forms and sizes, enabling you to express your creativity. Traditional pillar molds, silicone molds, and glass containers all provide distinct options for candle creation. Consider the sort of candles you want to make, then experiment with various molds and containers to get a variety of attractive designs.

Thermometer & Heat Source

Maintaining the appropriate temperature is critical throughout the candle-making process. A trustworthy thermometer allows you to monitor the wax temperature, ensuring that it melts uniformly and follows safety rules. Additionally, a continuous heat source, such as a double boiler or a specialized wax melting pot, helps to achieve a smooth and homogeneous wax consistency.

Navigating Authenticity And Regulations

Understanding the legal issues and rules governing candle manufacture is critical to ensuring smooth and compliant company operations. Compliance not only protects your company, but it also safeguards your consumers' safety.

Product Labeling

Proper labeling is a regulatory requirement for candles. Include important details such as the kind of wax used, aroma components, burning directions, and safety measures. Accurate and visible labeling fosters consumer confidence while also ensuring that your candles satisfy regulatory requirements.

CHAPTER THREE

Safety Standards And Tests

Candles must meet safety criteria to avoid accidents and risks. Conduct extensive testing to guarantee that your candles meet or surpass safety standards. This involves testing for the appropriate wick size, flame height, and burn duration. Keeping thorough records of these tests can help you not only comply with requirements but also solve any problems that may develop.

Intellectual Property Considerations

If you produce distinctive candle designs or smells, you should think about safeguarding your intellectual property. Trademarks may protect your brand, while patents may apply to innovative production techniques or unique candle formulas. A legal specialist specialized in intellectual property can help you navigate this complicated terrain.

Creating Your Unique Candle Designs

The visual attractiveness of your candles might help your business stand out in a competitive market. Developing distinctive designs requires a combination of imagination, talent, and attention to detail.

Experimenting With Shapes And Textures.

Experiment with unique forms and textures for your candles. Silicone molds allow for more detailed patterns, and additions like as glitter or botanicals may provide texture and visual appeal. Let your imagination go wild as you discover new candle aesthetics.

Custom Labels And Packaging

In addition to the candles, designing labels and packaging gives your items a unique touch. Spend time producing eye-catching labels that represent your brand's identity. Consider environmentally friendly packaging choices to meet the rising demand for sustainable goods.

Incorporating Personalized Elements

Consider selling customized candles that include components like initials, names, or unique messages. This not only increases emotional value for clients, but also makes your candles appropriate for special events such as weddings, birthdays, and anniversaries. Personalization may be an effective marketing tactic for targeting a specific market.

Cost And Pricing Strategies For Profitability

Setting the correct rates for your candles is critical to maintaining and expanding your candle-making company. Understanding your expenses and applying efficient pricing strategies enables profitability while maintaining quality.

Calculating Production Costs

Effective pricing is built on accurate manufacturing cost calculation. Consider all expenditures, such as raw materials, packaging, labor, utilities, and overhead costs. This comprehensive strategy guarantees that your price addresses all elements of manufacturing while maintaining an acceptable profit margin.

CHAPTER FOUR

Market Analysis And Competitive Pricing

Conduct extensive market research to better understand price trends and customer preferences. Analyze rivals' pricing methods to help you position your product competitively. Offering a combination of quality and price helps attract a larger client base, particularly in a market with diverse budget preferences.

Wholesale And Retail Pricing

If you want to sell your candles via both wholesale and retail channels, create unique price structures for each. Wholesale pricing often entails giving discounts to merchants that buy in bulk. Make sure your retail pricing cover manufacturing expenses, and wholesale discounts, and allow for a profit margin.

Building Your Candle-Making Workspace

Creating an efficient and tidy workstation is critical to optimizing your candle-making process. A well-equipped and organized workstation leads to higher productivity and a safer working environment.

Dedicated Work Area

Set aside a dedicated location for your candlemaking activity. Having a clear workplace, whether it's a room, a portion of a bigger space, or a separate studio, helps you concentrate and stay organized. This separation also reduces the potential of cross-contamination between various materials while providing a dedicated place for creativity.

Proper Ventilation

Making candles requires melting wax and dealing with scents, both of which may emit fumes. Maintain a healthy and pleasant working environment by ensuring appropriate airflow. Good ventilation also helps to improve air quality, particularly when dealing with various kinds of wax and perfumes.

Storage & Organization

Efficient storage and organizing are critical to a seamless operation. Invest in storage options for your equipment, materials, and completed items. This not only lowers clutter but also makes it simpler to find goods quickly, saving time throughout the candle-making process.

Safety Measures

Make safety a priority in your workplace by putting in place the required precautions. This includes having a first-aid kit, a fire extinguisher, and well-defined emergency protocols. Make sure your workstation conforms with local safety laws to establish a safe atmosphere for yourself and anybody else participating in the candlemaking process.

To summarize, mastering the art of candle manufacturing requires a mix of artistic flare, legal compliance, successful pricing methods, and a well-organized workplace.

You may take your candle-making business to the next level by investing in necessary equipment and materials, managing legalities, producing distinctive designs, applying cost-effective pricing, and constructing a practical workplace. Whether you're manufacturing candles for personal pleasure or starting a company, these fundamental ideas will help you succeed in the candle-making industry.

CHAPTER FIVE
Sourcing Supplies: A Guide For Smart Businesses

In the competitive world of candle enterprises, success is dependent not only on producing high-quality goods but also on strategic supply procurement. A well-thought-out raw material procurement strategy may have a major influence on your venture's overall efficiency and profitability. This book will throw light on the important issues and tactics for effectively acquiring materials for your candle company.

Understanding Your Needs

Before beginning the supplier selection process, it is critical to have a thorough grasp of your company's supply requirements. Consider the sorts of candles you make, the amounts needed, and the precise ingredients required for your unique product line. By providing a comprehensive picture of your needs, you will be better able to locate providers that share your company objectives.

Prioritize Quality Above Cost

While economic concerns are crucial in any organization, emphasizing quality above cost when purchasing supplies is vital to long-term success. High-quality materials help to create outstanding candles, which improves your brand's reputation and consumer happiness. Seek vendors that deliver consistent quality, even if it means paying a somewhat higher upfront cost; the long-term advantages will surpass the initial outlay.

Establishing Relationships With Suppliers

Building solid connections with suppliers is an essential component of effective procurement. Create open communication channels and develop a collaborative alliance. Reliable suppliers that understand your company requirements may give useful insights, keep you up to date on industry developments, and even provide special bargains. Long-term connections often provide preferential treatment and early access to new items.

Diversifying Suppliers For Resilience

Relying on a single supplier may offer considerable risks to your company, particularly if that supplier has difficulties or goes out of business. Diversifying your supplier base reduces these risks and provides a consistent supply of resources. Identify numerous suppliers for each essential commodity, evaluate their dependability, and devise backup plans for any possible supply chain interruptions.

Effective Marketing Strategies For Candle Businesses

Crafting amazing candles is just half the fight; efficiently marketing your goods is also critical to company success. With so many candle companies competing for customer attention, creative marketing may help you stand out and promote long-term success.

Identifying Your Unique Selling Proposition (USP).

Before you start marketing, identify your Unique Selling Proposition (USP). How do your candles stand out? A clear USP, whether it's the usage of high-quality materials, distinct smells, or environmentally sustainable activities, can assist frame your marketing messaging and attract the appropriate demographic.

27

Leveraging Social Media Platforms

In the digital era, social media networks are essential tools for promoting handcrafted goods. Create visually engaging material to showcase your candles on networks such as Instagram and Pinterest. Engage your audience by providing behind-the-scenes peeks into your creative process and promoting user-generated material. Social media not only increases brand awareness but also creates a feeling of community among your consumers.

Collaborations And Cross-Promotions

Collaborating with influencers, artists, or related companies might help you expand your marketing reach. Consider cross-promotions that benefit both companies by increasing your audience and presenting your products to new customers. Strategic relationships may also boost your brand's reputation, particularly if you link with influencers who share your beliefs.

Online Platforms for Selling Your Handcrafted Candles

The internet environment offers several options for candle enterprises to reach a worldwide audience. Using online channels to sell handmade candles might help you grow your market presence and boost sales.

CHAPTER SIX

Setting Up An E-Commerce Website

Developing a user-friendly e-commerce website is a critical step for any candle company seeking to build an online presence. Make sure your website is visually attractive, simple to browse, and offers safe payment methods. Invest in high-quality product photos and provide informative product descriptions to improve your clients' online buying experience.

Utilizing Online Marketplaces

In addition to having your website, you might sell your candles on prominent online markets like Etsy or Amazon Handmade. These platforms already have a large client base looking for handcrafted and distinctive items. Increase exposure by optimizing your product listings with relevant keywords, high-quality photos, and appealing product descriptions.

Customer Engagement And Developing A Loyal Following

Building a loyal client base is critical to long-term success in the candle company. Beyond delivering outstanding goods, increasing client interaction is critical to building long-term connections and driving repeat business.

Personalized Customer Interactions.

Spend time developing individualized encounters with your consumers. Respond quickly to queries, show thanks for purchases, and consider providing handwritten notes with your shipments. Making a personal connection with consumers improves their whole experience and motivates them to become dedicated advocates for your business.

Implementing A Reward Program

Introduce an incentive scheme to encourage repeat purchases. Rewards systems help clients feel valued and appreciated by offering discounts, exclusive access to new items, or a points-based system. This not only improves client retention but also promotes word-of-mouth recommendations.

Collecting And Utilizing Customer Feedback

Actively seek and utilize client input to enhance your goods and services. Positive evaluations may be effective marketing tools, whilst constructive criticism gives vital feedback for improvement. Consider using feedback surveys to demonstrate to clients that their views are important to the growth and development of your company.

To summarize, success in the candle industry requires a diversified strategy that goes beyond the creating process. Smart supply procurement, efficient marketing methods, and creating a loyal client base are all interwoven components that contribute to your company's long-term success. By adopting these principles, you may position your candle company for long-term development in a competitive industry.

Managing Finances And Budgeting For Growth

Successful financial management is critical for the success of any firm, including the candlemaking sector. A well-thought-out financial plan is critical for maintaining and growing your candle-making company. Begin by creating a complete budget that covers all parts of your business, from raw material purchases to marketing costs.

Consider introducing software or technologies that can automate financial procedures and provide insights into cash flow, costs, and earnings. Regularly evaluate and update your budget, changing it to reflect market changes or unanticipated obstacles. Maintaining a tight grasp on your money prepares your candle-making firm for long-term success.

Scaling Up: Growing Your Candle-Making Business

As your candle company grows, scaling up becomes inevitable. Scaling means increasing your manufacturing capacity, entering new markets, and improving your whole company infrastructure.

Careful preparation is required to guarantee a seamless transition during this vital time.

Investigate possibilities to improve manufacturing efficiency and reduce costs. Investigate new markets by performing market research and finding possible client segments. Consider partnerships or collaborations that can help you expand. Scaling up, whether via equipment upgrades or recruiting more employees, requires a systematic strategy to maintain candle quality while serving growing demand.

CHAPTER SEVEN
Overcoming The Challenges
Of Candle Entrepreneurship

Entrepreneurship in the candle-making sector is not without its hurdles. From acquiring excellent resources to negotiating market changes, resilience is essential for overcoming challenges. Identify foreseeable issues in advance and create contingency measures to lessen their effect.

Market rivalry, shifting customer tastes, and unexpected economic downturns are all regular issues for the candle sector. Keep up with industry developments and be ready to adjust your strategy appropriately. Developing a network inside the sector may give useful insights and assistance during difficult times. Taking a proactive approach can help you negotiate the intricacies of entrepreneurship in the candlemaking industry.

Triumph Story And Lessons Learned

Every great candle entrepreneur has had a unique road full of successes and losses. Highlighting success stories might motivate others and provide vital advice for prospective candlemakers. Share your experiences, including effective techniques and lessons learned from mistakes.

Interviewing successful entrepreneurs in the candle business may give a variety of viewpoints and ideas. Learn from their successes and struggles, and apply what you've learned to your company strategy. Success stories are not only motivational but also practical guidance for navigating the competitive terrain of the candlemaking industry.

Celebrate Milestones:
Reflections On Your Journey

As your candle-making firm reaches new milestones, take time to reflect on the experience. Celebrate accomplishments, large and small, since they represent development and growth. Milestones might include meeting a sales goal, entering new markets, or being recognized for product innovation.

Reflecting on your experience enables you to determine what went well and what needs to be improved. It's a chance to thank your staff and consumers who have contributed to your success. Use these observations to establish new goals and objectives for the future, ensuring that your candle-making company grows and thrives.

Conclusion

To summarize, managing money, scaling up, conquering problems, sharing success stories, and celebrating milestones are all interwoven factors that contribute to the overall development and success of your candle-making company. By taking a deliberate and proactive approach to each area, you may create a robust and flourishing business in the competitive candle market. As you navigate the ever-changing environment of candle entrepreneurship, be devoted to innovation, continual learning, and creating a great corporate culture.